S0-ASF-607

DIARY
OF A
MINECRAFT
SPIDER

BOOKS KID

TABLE OF CONTENTS

Day 1

Blinking my eyes, I stretched out a leg. Then another leg. Then another.

Uncurling my body, I stood up and counted all my legs.

One, two, three, four, five, six, seven, eight. That was a lot of legs!

Patting my face, I accidentally poked myself in the eye. Luckily, I had seven other eyes, so I could close that one to stop it watering and still see.

"I always love watching newly spawned spiders," chuckled a voice from across the room. Looking over, I could see another eight legged beastie. "You guys are always so hilarious when you try to figure out how to coordinate all your legs to move."

I went to take a step towards the spider, crossed my front legs and went crashing down to the ground.

"See what I mean?" it laughed. "Here. Let me help you. Pick up that leg at the front *first* and move the opposite leg at the back at the same time. Now the other front leg. That's right. You've got it!"

With the spider's help, I soon mastered the art of walking and even scuttling. I could climb up walls!

Full of the joy of being alive, I raced around the room, running high up the walls before bounding down and over to the opposite wall.

"Take it easy," warned the spider. "It's very easy to get carried away and then you'll be hit by an overwhelming hunger, and it will feel like there isn't enough food in the world to fill the void in your stomach."

"Thanks for the warning," I said, thinking that I could just do with a nice snack. "But who on earth are you?"

"Sorry. Didn't I introduce myself earlier?"

"No. You just laughed at me when I fell over."

"Did I?" The spider shook its head. "How rude of me. My name is Zed. And your name is Boris."

"What do you mean, my name is Boris? Don't I get to pick my name?"

"Nope." The spider shook its head again, more vehemently this time. "It's a tradition among spiders that the first spider to see you after spawning gets to pick your name. It's another reason I like to hang out around the spawner. I like the idea that there are hundreds of spiders running around Minecraftia with names that I gave them."

"Boris…" I said the name slowly, liking the way it sounded. "Boris I am, then!"

Day 2

I peered cautiously around the corner of the door. It had taken me a long time to work up the courage to leave the room I was spawned in, but after Zed had disappeared off a while back to go and find something to eat, I'd waited and waited for him to return. That had been hours ago and there was still no sign of him. Meanwhile, my stomach was rumbling and I was starving! Zed was right – run around too much and you really will feel as though no food could ever fill the bottomless void that was your stomach!

The door opened onto a corridor that went left and right. I looked in both directions to see if there was any clue where Zed had gone, but there was no sign of him.

I stood there, unsure of what to do. I was all alone. What happened if I met a monster? What if there were lots of traps out there? I was too young to die!

In the end, I decided to spin a thread, attaching one end to the door of the dungeon. That way, I'd be able to find my way back if I came across something scary and could hide in one of the chests in the dungeon.

Proud of myself for coming up with such a brilliant plan, I quickly secured a rope to the door and headed off down the corridor. What wonders would I find out in the big wide world? More importantly, what food could I get? If I didn't eat something soon, I felt as though I would wither away from starvation and there couldn't be a more pathetic sight than a famished spider.

Day 3

Turning the corner, the corridor opened up into a room and I almost dropped my silk thread when I saw the strange creature in there. They had four legs, but they were standing on just two of them, using the other two to carry a bag and a sword.

I'd never imagined that anything could be so ugly. A shiver of disgust ran through me at the sight. I guessed that this must be a human. Zed had mentioned them to me when we were talking. Apparently, they were notorious thieves. They went through dungeons and mines, stealing everything that wasn't nailed down – and even when resources *were* secured, they still went out of their way to take whatever they could get.

Still, I didn't have anything worth stealing, so as long as the human left me alone, I didn't see why we had to have a problem with each other.

I crept into the room, keeping to the outskirts to stay as far away from the human as possible. I didn't want its nasty, smooth skin to touch me. The very idea made me shudder.

The human gazed at me as I walked around it and I stared back. If it wanted to have a staring contest, then it was game on!

The human's eyes widened when it realized that I wasn't afraid of it, and it backed away from me. Good. I was glad that it recognized that I was a threat. As long as it didn't work out that I was more afraid of it than it was of me, everything would be just fine.

As the human edged backwards, its elbow caught one of the torches hanging on the wall, knocking it down and plunging it into darkness.

"How dare you!" I roared, enraged. I was terrified of the dark! The human must have known that and made the room dark on purpose. I briefly considered running away, but I wasn't going to risk having the human come after me and attack me when I least expected it. After all, the best form of defense is a good offense, and if the human wanted a fight, I was going to make sure that I finished it.

I was surprised to discover how well I could see in the dark and I spotted the human immediately as it waved its sword around to keep me at bay. The first thing I needed to do was disarm it, so I launched myself at its arm, aiming a kick at its elbow.

My attack landed perfectly and the human dropped the sword, clutching its arm in agony. Taking advantage of my success, I rained blows down on its face and body, moving too quickly for it to be able to fight back.

The human managed to block some of my punches, but I was just too fast for it and it wasn't long before it was lying on the ground, defeated.

"Take that!" I crowed, picking up the torch and carrying it to the nearest lit torch to rekindle it, restoring the light to the room. I scuttled over to the human to take a closer look. Those things really are disgusting!

"That'll teach you to try and frighten a spider," I jeered, kicking the human in the ribs to make sure that it wasn't getting up. It didn't move. I'd won my first fight!

Spotting the human's bag, I wondered what it had been carrying, so I sorted through the contents. Most of it was useless. Shiny metals, bottles with strange liquid inside, clothing that would never fit on a spider in a million years.

However, I got lucky when I reached the bottom of the bag. Food!

I didn't care what it was. I didn't even stop to think about whether a spider should be eating human food. I was so hungry that I wolfed it down, barely even taking a moment to look at what I was eating.

I have to say that human food isn't bad at all. I had no idea what it was that I'd eaten, but it tasted pretty good and I felt all refreshed and ready to tackle the next challenge that came along. If there were any other humans in the dungeons thinking about snuffing out the torches, they'd better watch out!

Day 4

I'd explored a lot of the tunnels leading away from the room I was spawned in, but there was still no sign of Zed. I wondered what had happened to him. Maybe he'd been defeated by a human!

I hoped not. Zed was the only other spider I'd ever met. If he was gone, I was all alone in the world, the last of my kind.

I sniffed, a solitary tear running down my cheek at the idea that there were no other spiders in the dungeons.

"What's wrong?"

I whirled round at the sound of someone behind me and saw a spider.

"Zed!" I beamed. "I'm so glad to see you."

"Sorry, but you must be confused," the spider said. "I'm not Zed. I'm Fang."

"Fang?"

"Let me guess – you're newly spawned?" The spider smiled kindly. "Don't worry. Come with me and I'll introduce you to the other spiders. I know how overwhelming it can be when you first spawn and you don't know anyone."

The spider beckoned to me to follow as it headed off down a corridor. I couldn't wait to see where Fang was taking me. I wasn't alone after all – I was going to meet my spider family!

Day 5

"There's a whole colony of spiders that live in the dungeons," Fang explained. "Although most spiders decide that they want to explore the world after a while. It can get a bit boring running around the same four walls all the time. They always come back here eventually, though. There's no place like home!"

"Have you left the dungeons, then?" I asked.

"Not yet." Fang shook his head. "I like it down here. Yes, sometimes I think I might like a change of scenery, but then I listen to some of the stories the other spiders have told and decide that I'm better off in the dungeons. It's dangerous out in Minecraftia! Do you know how many spiders get attacked out there by humans? It's as though they're afraid of us or something. How stupid is that? Don't they know that we're far more scared of them, and with good reason? The only reason we'd attack a human would be because they'd turned out the lights and no spider likes to be in the dark, but humans are weird and unpredictable. They'll attack us without any provocation. As far as I'm concerned, the fewer humans I see, the better and I know lots of good places to hide in the dungeons. I can't remember the last time I've been around a human."

"I fought one a couple of days ago," I told him proudly.

"Really? You're lucky to be alive then. Those things are vicious!" Fang spat. "Anyway, enough about humans. It's time you met your family. Welcome to Spider World!"

He motioned for me to go ahead and I couldn't believe what I saw. A room filled with spiders, far too many to count! Far from being the only one of my kind, I had cousins, uncles, aunts, brothers and sisters, all waiting to get to know me!

"Wow." It was the only thing I could think of to say.

Day 6

"What's your name?"

The spider asking dangled upside down in front of my face, showing off his web spinning skills.

"Boris," I replied.

"Boris?" sneered the spider. "What a stupid name! Why did you pick that?"

"I didn't pick it. Zed named me," I explained.

"Why did you let Zed name you? He always chooses dumb names."

"I didn't *let* Zed name me," I protested. "He told me that the first spider you see after you've been spawned gets to decide your name. It's spider tradition."

"He fed you that heap of garbage and you believed him?" laughed the spider. "Jeepers! You're even more stupid than you look."

"What do you mean?"

"We're *spiders*!" The spider rolled its eight eyes. "Nobody tells us what to do and nobody tells us what we should be calling ourselves. We choose our own names and Boris is the worst name I've ever heard."

"Oh really?" I lifted my chin, trying not to let the spider know that it was upsetting me. "So what's your name, then, if you're such a genius?"

"Gilbert," came the surprising reply.

"Gilbert?" I stifled a giggle. If I didn't want someone to laugh at my name, then I shouldn't make fun of theirs, but that really *was* a ridiculous sounding name.

"Yes. It means 'bright pledge,'" Gilbert informed me. "It's an ancient name, only taken by the very bravest."

"How on earth do you know where your name comes from?"

I was treated to another one of Gilbert's sneering looks. "From the *Big Book of Spider Names* of course. We all use it when we're deciding what to call ourselves." He sniffed. "Well, by all of us who have the sense we're born with and don't just believe whatever anyone tells us."

"So what does Boris mean?" I asked, intrigued. Zed must have chosen my name for a reason and I didn't understand why Gilbert thought it was such a bad choice.

"Go look it up for yourself."

Gilbert pulled himself up his thread and scurried away, leaving me wondering where I could find this book.

Day 7

"Hey, Fang. I've been looking all over for you. Where've you been?" I ran up to Fang, delighted that I'd finally found him.

"Hi, Boris. I've just been checking the spawners to see if there are any new spiders. What's wrong?"

"It's not something wrong exactly." I blushed and scuffed at the floor, feeling suddenly embarrassed about having fallen for Zed's story.

"Come on, Boris. You can tell me."

"Where's the *Big Book of Spider Names*?" I blurted out.

"Why? You already have a name, don't you?"

"I do. It's just…"

"Let me guess. Gilbert has been making fun of you."

I said nothing, nodding glumly.

"You don't want to pay any attention to what Gilbert says. He's just a mean spider. He's always looking for ways to make other people feel bad. I keep saying that he should leave the dungeons and go explore the world. A bit of experience in other cultures would teach him to be a little more understanding of spiders who are different."

"But that's just it!" I cried. "I didn't think that my name was different. I thought it was a perfectly good name. I thought Zed named lots of spiders."

"He did," nodded Fang. "That Zed has got a lot to answer for. He's done this plenty of times. He finds a newly spawned spider and then persuades them to let him give them a silly name."

"But what's so silly about Boris?" I asked. "I like the sound of it."

"Come with me." Fang turned and trotted off towards a small antechamber I hadn't noticed before. "There." He pointed to a book lying on a table. "The *Big Book of Spider Names*. Read it and see for yourself why Boris isn't a very popular name around here."

I crept towards the table. For a so-called 'big' book, it was surprisingly small. Picking it up, I flicked through the pages until I came to the letter B.

"Bert… Bob… Ah, here we are. Boris. It means wolf." I looked up at Fang. "That doesn't seem so strange."

"Wolves are the natural enemies of spiders," Fang explains. "I've lost count of how many friends I've lost to the jaws of a wolf. Giving you that name was like hanging a sign around your neck that says *Kick Me*. No spider would choose that name for themselves."

"I see." I bit my lip, struggling to hold back tears.

"You can choose another name for yourself if you like," offered Fang. "Spiders don't usually change their names, but under the circumstances, nobody would mind."

"NO!" The word came out more forcefully than I intended. "I *like* the sound of Boris. I don't care if it's got a bad meaning. I'm going to show the other spiders that it doesn't matter what name you have. I'm going to make Boris the most popular name in the world!"

"That's the spirit," smiled Fang.

"But in the meantime, I'm going to find Zed and give him a piece of my mind. That was a mean trick to play on a newly spawned spider."

"When you find him, tell him I want to see him as well, will you?" asked Fang. "Nobody has seen him for days and you're not the only spider he's upset recently."

"I will," I promised, little knowing how difficult it would be to track him down.

Day 8

"Have you seen Zed?" I asked.

"Seen him? I haven't even heard of him." The spider marched off, leaving me no closer to finding Zed. I'd spoken to what felt like every spider in the dungeon and nobody knew where he was.

"What's wrong, Boris?"

My heart sank when I saw Gilbert coming towards me.

"Have you realized what a lousy name you've been lumbered with?" he sneered.

"There's nothing wrong with my name," I protested. "If you met a wolf, you'd run away, screaming like a baby. Wolves are fearsome fighters, so you'd better watch yourself or you'll find out for yourself just how tough we are."

"Oh yeah? You and what army?" Gilbert strode towards me menacingly.

"That's enough, Gilbert!"

We both jumped as Fang came to stand between us. "I've told you before to not make fun of people's names. Or do I need to remind you of the name Zed gave you?"

"Zed gave him a name?" A grin spread across my face. "What was it?"

"Don't tell him, Fang!" begged Gilbert.

Fang sighed. "Just be a little kinder, all right?"

"I will," promised Gilbert.

"Come on. What did Zed call you?" I urged Gilbert after Fang had left.

"I'm never going to tell you. And if you even mention to anyone that I had another name, I'll find you, do you hear?" threatened Gilbert. The venom in his voice told me that he meant what he was saying, so I didn't say anything, just nodded to let him know that I understood.

Day 9

I'd looked everywhere in the spider caves and there was no sign of Zed. If I wanted to tell him what I thought of him for tricking me, then I had no choice. I was going to have to leave the dungeons and go out into Minecraftia and see if I could find him there.

It was a scary thought. All I'd ever known were the dungeons and the network of tunnels and caves the spiders had carved out for themselves over the years. I had no idea what could be waiting for me out in the big, wide world.

"You look like you're thinking about something very serious," observed Fang, coming to sit next to me.

"I'm thinking about Zed."

"Wondering why he gave you the name he did?"

"No. Well, yes. I do wonder why he gives new spiders silly names, but that wasn't what I was thinking about just then. I've looked all over the spider network and there's no sign of him. I think he's gone out into Minecraftia. I was considering going out after him."

"Really?" Fang whistled. "You're a braver spider than I am, then. I'd never leave the tunnels. It's far too dangerous out there. Minecraftia is stuffed full of humans. Nasty creatures." He shuddered and so did I. We all hated humans.

"That's what's putting me off from going," I confessed. "I'm just one spider and the world is a scary place. At the same time, I want to know what's happened to Zed. Why did he leave like that? Did he give one stupid name too many? Did he decide to go and find another spawner? Or has something more sinister happened to him? Maybe he's been spidernapped!"

Fang laughed. "I don't think anyone would want to take Zed away. He's not exactly the most hard-working of spiders and nobody is going to pay a ransom to get him back. What would be the point of spidernapping him?"

"Perhaps they haven't done it for a ransom," I suggested. "Perhaps they just wanted to save other spiders from being called Boris or…" I pretended to think, an innocent expression on my face. "What was it Gilbert used to be called? He did tell me, but I've forgotten."

"Nice try," chuckled Fang, "but I promised Gilbert I wasn't going to tell anyone and I keep my promises."

"Oh well. You can't blame a spider for trying," I shrugged. "But don't you want to know what happened to Zed?"

"Not really." Fang shook his head. "Spiders come and go all the time. I really don't think that anything suspicious has happened. Zed obviously decided that he was going to move on. Are you really so desperate to know why he called you Boris that you're going to risk going outside after him?"

I thought for a moment. "Maybe not, but I'm going to follow him anyway. Something is not right here and I'm determined to get to the bottom of it."

Day 10

I stood in front of the exit from the spider caves. This was the moment of truth. Outside that trapdoor lay Minecraftia, filled with danger and monsters.

For a moment, I considered going back. Fang was probably right. Zed had his fun and had gone to find another dungeon to live in.

Yet something inside me said that there was a problem and Zed was in danger. Just because he had played a trick on me didn't mean that he didn't deserve rescuing. If I left and found that he was safely living in another dungeon, then at least I'd have had some adventures to talk about. Nobody would make fun of my name if I'd fought off an entire gang of Minecraftians single-handedly.

But if he *was* in danger, then it was my duty as a fellow spider to rescue him. I was going to prove that it didn't matter what name you were given. Every spider had the potential to be a hero.

Taking a deep breath, I plucked up my courage and reached forward to open the trap door. As it flipped out, sunlight flooded in, forcing me to cover my eyes so they wouldn't get hurt from the sudden bright light.

At last, my eyes had adjusted and I was able to peek out of the trapdoor. I couldn't believe what I saw.

Minecraftia was beautiful! So many colors, so many sounds, so many smells!

Pulling myself out of the spider tunnels, I stood on grass for the first time in my life. Lifting up each of my legs, I loved the way the green stuff gave way beneath my feet.

Now that I was outside, I never wanted to go back in the tunnels again. I couldn't understand why the spiders didn't move out here. It was the most amazing place I'd ever seen.

Day 11

I ambled through the forest, mouth open in awe as I took in the sights. When you're spawned in a dim, dingy dungeon, it's difficult to imagine how stunning the outside world could be. The sun was shining, the birds were singing and it was as perfect a day as could be.

Wait. When I said the sun was shining, what I should have said was that it was pouring with rain! No sooner had I closed my eyes to soak up some rays, when I was hit straight in the face with a load of raindrops!

Nobody had warned me about rain and I was drenched before I could take shelter. Sopping wet, I climbed up the nearest tree and took shelter among the leaves, huddled against the trunk while I waited for the rain to pass.

However, even in the rain, Minecraftia was still lovely. In fact, the rain added a bluish tinge that made everything sparkle and glow. Not even rain could dampen my spirits.

Day 12

GROAN!

I'd had to wait until after dark for the rain to stop and I was eager to get moving and track down Zed, but now that it was dim, my natural fear of the dark returned. If that was a human I heard, I was going to bite him until there was nothing left!

Well, I probably wouldn't do that. But I *would* attack him before he attacked me. You never could be too careful and everyone knew that humans were to be feared.

GROAN!

I heard a rustling in the bushes nearby and I crouched, ready to spring forward at the human making its way towards me.

GROAN!

A person lurched through the bushes, but just as I was about to leap into action, some instinct told me to hang back. Looking more closely at the humanoid, I noticed that its skin wasn't the usual ugly pink color. Instead, it was an eerie green.

Furthermore, it didn't smell the same as a normal human. There was a distinct odor of rotting flesh coming from it.

Something wasn't right here.

"Excuse me?" I cleared my throat when the creature didn't reply. "I said, excuse me?"

"Ug?"

The thing turned its head towards me.

"I'm looking for a spider named Zed. Have you seen him?"

"Blarg?"

"Do you speak English?"

"Groan!" The being nodded its head.

"So you understand what I'm saying?"

"Groan!" Another nod.

"So can you help me find my friend?"

"Ug!" The thing shrugged.

"Have you seen a spider called Zed?"

"Groan!"

This was pointless. The thing seemed to understand what I was saying, but I didn't have a clue what he was trying to tell me.

"Can. You. Speak. English?"

"Groan!" The monster nodded enthusiastically, but I still couldn't make out any words.

Then the mystery was solved. The creature opened its mouth and its jaw fell off! It scrabbled around on the floor to find it, pushing it back into place with a click.

"Wait a minute!" I gasped. "I know what you are! You're a zombie!"

"Uh-huh," nodded the zombie.

I'd been wasting my time. Everyone knew that zombies had no brains. It's why they were constantly looking for human brains to replace the intelligence they'd lost. While this one might be able to understand what I was asking it, it wouldn't be able to help me find Zed. It was just too stupid.

"Could you maybe show me where spiders go when they come to the forest?" I asked. It was a long shot, but maybe the zombie could at least give me some idea where to go next to find Zed.

"Ug." The zombie pointed to the left.

"Thank you!" I made to go off to the left, when the zombie put out a hand to stop me.

"Ug," nodded the zombie, pointing to the right. Then it pointed up and down.

"Great," I sighed. "Thanks for your time."

"Groan!" The zombie shuffled off, leaving me no closer to discovering what had happened to Zed.

Day 13

After walking all night, I was exhausted, but I hadn't lost hope. I knew that Zed was somewhere in this forest. I just needed to figure out where.

Curling up underneath a tree, I decided to take a rest for a while. Closing my eyes, I figured that it wouldn't hurt to take a little nap to refresh myself.

Just as I was nodding off, THUNK!

An arrow embedded itself in the trunk of the tree I was leaning against.

"Oh, I am so sorry. I didn't see you there. Are you all right?"

A skeleton came rushing up to me, what seemed like a worried expression on its face. It was hard to tell. It was a skeleton and skulls aren't known for being highly expressive.

I patted myself down.

"I seem to be OK," I replied. "The arrow hit the tree."

"That one did," said the skeleton. "But this one didn't."

I paled when the skeleton pointed to an arrow sticking out of the ground, a couple of centimeters away from where my leg had been. That was a little too close for comfort.

"I'll go and find another place for target practice," the skeleton told me.

"Wait!" I called as it turned to move away. "Maybe you can help me."

"I'll certainly try."

"I'm looking for a friend of mine. His name is Zed. He's about my size, grey and black with red eyes. Have you seen him?"

"I have no idea," apologized the skeleton. "I might have seen him, but I wouldn't know. All you spiders look the same to me. I have seen some spiders coming through here, but I couldn't say whether any of them were called Zed."

"Some spiders is better than none," I smiled. "Which way were they going?"

"They were going in different directions, but most of them were heading off that way."

The skeleton pointed to the east.

"Thanks a lot," I beamed. "That's a huge help."

"No problem. I hope you find who you're looking for," the skeleton called after me as I hurried along to catch up with the spiders he'd seen. Hopefully one of them would be Zed.

Day 14

I'd been moving as fast as I could, but I still hadn't seen any sign of any other spiders. However, I realized that I hadn't asked the skeleton *when* he'd last seen the spiders. I could still be a good few days behind them, so I needed to hurry if I was going to catch up with them.

A noise sent me scurrying for the shelter of the bushes. I crouched beneath the leaves as a group of Minecraftians came marching down the road.

"How far away did you say the witch's hut was?"

"Not far. The swamp is only a couple of days away and the hut's near the outskirts."

"And you reckon we can beat her easily?"

"Come on! She's just one witch and there's five of us. She won't stand a chance, especially with my enchanted sword. We'll have more potions than we could ever use once we're finished with her."

"After all, we destroyed that group of zombies we met the other night. One witch is going to be easy compared to that horde."

"True, true."

I held my breath as the Minecraftians walked past me, so close that I could have reached out a leg and touched them. Going by their boasts of all the creatures they killed, I didn't like to think about what might happen if they discovered me hiding so close.

"Wouldn't it be easier to brew our own potions?" asked a new voice. "I hate the fact that we're just fighting and stealing to get what we want."

"Brew our own potions?"

The other Minecraftians burst out laughing.

"Don't be so silly! Why would we go to all that trouble when someone else has already done the hard work? We get the potions from the witch so we don't have to waste our time and we can focus on having fun instead. I want to break the world record for the most zombies killed in one night and I can't do that if I don't have a wide range of splash potions to hand. We agreed that we were going to kill the witch – or at least injure her so she stays out of our way – and take her entire stash of potions. You're not getting cold feet are you?"

"No, no." The Minecraftian who had spoken up against fighting the witch was quick to deny that he was getting scared.

"Good. So that's settled. We find the witch, we defeat her and then we steal her potions. It's the perfect plan. What could go wrong?"

The Minecraftians carried on down the road and when I was sure that they were far enough away not to see me, I came out from underneath the bush.

If I'd ever needed any confirmation of the wickedness of humans, I'd had it. They were planning on fighting someone just so they could steal her things because they were too lazy to make their own potions.

Pure evil.

It was a good thing that I'd stayed away from the humans. I didn't want to think what they might have done to me if they'd found my hiding place.

Day 15

I felt as though I'd been walking forever. My feet were covered in blisters and there were blisters on top of my blisters. My poor feet would probably never recover.

Would I ever find Zed? After all, nobody had been able to tell me which way he'd gone. Perhaps I'd been walking in the wrong direction all this time, getting further and further away from him.

"Oink!"

A peculiar looking beast came wandering through the trees. Maybe it could tell me where Zed was.

"Excuse me? Excuse me?"

The thing totally ignored me.

"Excuse me?" I tapped it hard on the back so there was no way it could miss my wanting to talk to it.

"Oink!" The thing glared at me before snorting and moving away. It didn't look like I was going to get any help from it.

Still, it wasn't the only woodland animal. Maybe I could find one that was more cooperative.

"Hello? Can you help me?"

I went up to a four legged creature with black and white spots.

"I'm looking for a spider called Zed. Have you seen him?"

"Moo!"

The thing took a large mouthful of grass and started chewing.

"I'm sorry. I didn't quite understand you. Did you say that you had seen my friend or you hadn't?"

"Moo!"

The beast didn't even bother looking at me as it slowly walked over to where it thought there was a juicy mouthful of grass.

"Can you help me? Please?"

There was a loud noise as the animal let rip the loudest fart I'd ever heard. A moment later, I realized that it was the smelliest fart I'd ever been around too. It was clear that I was wasting my time.

I'd never felt more alone in my life.

Day 16

I carried on down the road, keeping my eight eyes open for Minecraftians. One of the biggest advantages of having eight eyes was that I could see in all directions around me, so when I saw a Minecraftian coming towards me, I scuttled up a tree so that I could watch what they were doing and remain unseen.

This human looked different to the other adventurers I'd seen. I hadn't thought it possible, but it was even uglier than the other Minecraftians. It had a huge nose that was so long, it practically touched its chin. It was wearing a pointy hat and long, dark robes.

Disgusting! How can these humans ever look at themselves in the mirror? And how do they cope with just four limbs? No wonder they're all thieves and murderers. They've been driven mad by the lack of legs.

It was clear to me that spiders are the superior species. With our eight legs and eight eyes, we can see everything around us and don't have to rely on someone else warning us if something's creeping up and we can easily jump out of the way with hardly any effort.

I love being a spider.

As the human came close to my hiding place, it stopped, sniffing the air.

"Hmmm. Come to me, my pretty," I thought I heard it say. Was it talking to me? Well, if it was, it was going to be disappointed. I wasn't so easily fooled and I wasn't going to be tempted out of my hiding place, especially not for a human that was so ugly.

It sniffed a few more times and I hugged the tree trunk, hoping that I was camouflaged against it. If it realized that I was above it, I was an easy target for an archer.

I didn't even notice that I was holding my breath until the human finally moved away and I let it out. My heart was pumping at how close I'd come to being discovered by a Minecraftian.

I needed to find Zed and fast so that I could get us both to somewhere safe. I didn't really want to go back down into the dungeons now that I'd experienced the wonders of Minecraftia, but if that was the only place where spiders wouldn't be persecuted by humans, then perhaps it was the best place for all of us.

Day 17

I heard the sound of fighting up ahead and I dithered, wondering what the best thing to do would be. Was Zed fighting for his life? Or was it a scuffle between humans, something best avoided for my own safety?

I decided that I couldn't risk my own life, but I didn't want to leave Zed to fend for himself, so I ran up the nearest tree, spinning a web as I went. Using my silk to keep me off the ground, I swung from tree to tree, hidden from any humans on the ground.

At last, I reached the source of the noise and I was stunned at what I saw. The human with the pointy hat was fighting the gang of Minecraftians I'd hidden from the other day. One against five was hardly a fair fight, yet she seemed to be holding her own by throwing bottles at the Minecraftians. As they exploded against the humans, the five adventurers were clearly hurt by the contents, buying the solo human time to attack them.

As I watched, the potion throwing human gradually overcame her opponents as, one by one, they fell to the ground, unconscious. This must be the witch the adventurers had been talking about and it looked as though they had seriously underestimated her fighting skills.

I had to restrain myself from cheering when the final adventurer dropped his sword and ran away screaming from the witch. It served him right. The Minecraftians had planned on defeating the witch purely to save themselves some time. I hoped the witch's potions had caused them lots of painful damage so they'd think twice about ambushing someone again.

The witch made her way round all the fallen adventurers, helping herself to resources and equipment from their backpacks. When she was finished, she pulled herself upright, sniffing the air again.

"I know you're close, my pretty," she muttered to herself. "Soon you'll come to me. You won't be able to help yourself."

She looked around, but didn't seem to spot me hiding in the tree before she walked off down the road. Keeping a safe distance, I used my web to swing from tree to tree so that I could spy on her.

By the time night fell, I was satisfied that she wasn't any threat to me. At last, I'd finally found someone I could trust to help me in my quest.

Day 18

The next day, I followed the witch all morning and didn't see any sign of cruelty to animals. Unlike the adventurers, who'd slaughtered pigs and cows for food, the witch appeared to be vegetarian, which was another indication that she might be the first human I'd ever met who I didn't have to be afraid of.

When she sat down for some lunch, I decided that the moment had come to talk to her. Swinging down from the tree, I kept hold of my silk thread so that I could swing away if I was wrong about her.

"Hello?" I said timidly as the witch was about to take a bite out of a piece of pie.

Her head snapped up.

"Who's there?" she snapped.

"My name is Boris. Please don't be afraid," I told her, as I edged towards her.

"I'm not afraid of anything," sniffed the witch. "I've got plenty of potions to hand if you try anything stupid."

"Don't worry," I reassured her. "I'm not planning on doing anything silly. I'm just searching for a spider and I wondered if you might have seen him."

"A spider you say? What's his name?"

"Zed," I replied. "He's around my size, eight black legs-"

"Red eyes?" finished the witch.

"Yes!" I exclaimed. "His name is Zed. Have you seen him?"

"I have," nodded the witch.

"When? Where?"

"A few days ago," she told me. "In the swamp not too far from here. In fact, I was on my way there myself right now. I live there, you see, so I know whenever someone new moves into the area and I definitely remember your friend finding a hollow tree to live in. I can show you his new home if you like."

"Really?" I gasped, scarcely believing my luck. "You'd do that?"

"I'm going that way," shrugged the witch. "It's not exactly a big deal to take you to see your friend and, quite frankly, I'd rather show you which way to go than have you stomping all over my swamp, ruining my garden."

"Thank you! That's so kind of you," I gushed. "When can we leave?"

"Have some patience, can't you? I haven't even started my lunch. Can't a girl have some food without being bothered?"

"I'm sorry," I apologized. "It's just that you have no idea how much this means to me. I've been looking for Zed for so long and this is the first time I've been able to speak to someone who's seen him. I thought I was going to be wandering around this forest forever without ever finding him."

"Well, you would have done that if you hadn't met me," laughed the witch. "He hasn't been in the forest for ages. I must admit that I was surprised when he moved into the swamp. It's quite damp and a lot of spiders don't like getting their feet wet. But if you don't mind a bit of water, I can reunite you with your friend in just a few days."

"I don't mind at all," I smiled, hardly able to contain my excitement. Soon, I'd be able to uncover the secret behind why Zed chose my name and make sure that he'd never do the same to another newly spawned spider.

Day 19

"So how long have you lived in the swamp?" I asked as I trotted along next to the witch, whose name was Louise.

"All my life," came the reply. "I love living there. It's wonderfully peaceful. Nobody ever comes and bothers me." She glared at me and I cringed away.

"I'm sorry for intruding on you," I apologized for what seemed like the millionth time. Louise was a very touchy individual and it seemed as though she'd take offense at the slightest thing. "But once I've found Zed, we'll both be out of your swamp before you know it."

"Oh, Zed is no bother." She waved away my reassurances. "He stays in his hollow tree and doesn't bother me. Truth be told, I quite like having him there. He's like an early warning alarm system. Whenever an adventurer sees him, they always scream because he's so big. It gives me time to gather my potions together to give the adventurer a proper swamp 'welcome.'"

I laughed at the thought of a big, bold adventurer shrieking at the sight of a spider.

"So what's it like being a witch?" I asked her. "It sounds like it must be very exciting."

"Far too exciting if you ask me," sighed the witch. "People always assume the worst. Just because I live on my own in a swamp, brewing potions, Minecraftians think that I must be up to no good. I'm always having to fight people to get them to leave me alone."

"Like the adventurers you were fighting the other day," I nodded.

"So you *were* watching," exclaimed the witch. "I thought so. Why didn't you help me?"

"I'm sorry." There it was. Another apology. "I didn't know that you were a good person. I thought you were another evil Minecraftian."

"I suppose it's an easy mistake to make," sniffed the witch.

"But I know different now," I rushed to reassure her. "So if you were to get into another fight, I'd be right there by your side, fighting Minecraftians."

"That's good to know." Louise treated me to a rare smile. "I might just call on you to do that one of these days."

Day 20

The forest gave way to swamp and I discovered that the witch hadn't been lying when she said that my feet were going to get wet. I didn't understand how Zed could have chosen to live in such a damp place when the forest was so much nicer.

"Is Zed nearby?" I asked. "Is that his tree over there?"

Louise shook her head. "We've still got a way to go before we reach Zed's home. But don't worry. We're on the right track."

I saw some movement up ahead and I crouched down, ready to go on the attack to defend the witch.

"Stand down, soldier," laughed Louise. "That's Hyacinth. She's my friend. Stay here. I need to have a quick chat with her." She glared at me. "In private."

"Of course."

I settled down to wait for Louise as she picked her way through the boggy swamp to where another witch was waiting for her. The two of them started muttering and I saw them looking over at me a few times.

However, although they tried to keep their voices down, the one thing the witches didn't realize was how good spider hearing was. As the wind changed direction, it picked up their words, taking them in my direction. It took all my self-control to hide my shock and horror at what I heard.

"Yes, Hyacinth. It's just as I told you. Everything's going to plan. Soon I'll get my hands on a massive supply of spider eyes, plenty to keep us both going for months."

"I've seen your cages. You've got a decent number of spiders collected, but that's not going to be enough to make all the potions we've got planned."

"Who said anything about limiting ourselves to the spiders I've got locked up? I've just picked up a freshly spawned spider. It's wonderfully naïve. It's told me how to find the dungeon where its friends and family live and once I've captured him, I'm going to work my way through all the tunnels and caves the spiders have carved out for themselves and pick up every single spider lurking there. When I say that I'm going to have enough spider eyes to keep us going for months, I mean it."

"I like the way you think," the other witch cackled. "Those spiders won't know what's hit them."

"Anyway, you'd better go. I don't want Boris to get suspicious. I'll let you know when I'm planning on attacking the dungeon if you want to come and help."

"Sure."

The other witch disappeared off into the depths of the swamp and Louise came back over to me, smiling.

"Sorry about that," she said. "That Hyacinth is such a chatterbox! It's always hard to get her to stop talking once she starts."

"No problem," I smiled, but inside, my mind was whirling. Spider eyes! Attack the dungeon!

I'd been right to come after Zed. I'd uncovered a plot to wipe out my home colony. But I was just one spider. What could I do to stop Louise and her friend?

Day 21

"Is everything all right?" asked Louise, as we made our way through the swamp. "You seem very quiet."

"Oh, I'm just worried about Zed," I lied. "Living in a hollow tree must be very different to the warmth of the dungeon. I hope he's OK and getting enough to eat."

"I wouldn't worry about him," Louise reassured me. "Zed's a very resourceful spider. I bet that by the time you catch up with him, he'll amaze you with everything he's done. You two will have so much to talk about!"

"Do you see much of him?" I asked, careful not to let Louise know that I was really trying to get information about Zed and the other captive spiders.

"Why would I want to hang out with a horrible spider?" scoffed the witch, letting her act slip for a moment before remembering who she was talking to. "I mean, we don't have very much in common. He's a spider, I'm a witch… What would we chat about?"

"We're chatting now," I pointed out.

"Yes, but you're different. You're not like any spider I've ever met."

"What, you mean really naïve?" I muttered under my breath.

"What was that?" asked Louise sharply.

"Nothing!" I beamed, but inside I was hoping that we would get to the witch's home soon. The sooner I could rescue Zed and the others and get away with her, the better. I didn't want to spend a second more with her than I had to.

Day 22

"Here we are!" announced Louise. "Home, sweet home."

She pointed to a rundown shack up ahead. It looked like it could fall down at any second, but I plastered a bright smile on my face. "It looks lovely."

As we drew close, I tried to spot where the witch might be hiding Zed and the spiders. There were lots of dark nooks and crannies around the trees, but I couldn't see anything big enough to conceal a group of spiders.

"Where's Zed?" I asked.

"He'll be around somewhere," replied Louise vaguely. "Don't worry about him. He's probably off hunting for food. Speaking of which, why don't you come inside my hut and have a snack? You must be starving after all the walking we've been doing."

"Sure." My heart pounded in my chest as I followed the witch towards the hut. I was going to have to time this carefully if I was going to get as much information as possible out of her before escaping.

"Oh look!" exclaimed the witch. "Zed is inside my hut."

"Really? Where?"

"Just inside. Go closer and see for yourself."

I knew that Zed wasn't there. She had him locked up somewhere else, but I wanted to get a peek inside her hut just in case.

"Come on, my pretty. Go into my hut."

Louise put a hand on my back, pushing me towards her hut and I knew that I couldn't stick around any longer.

"Leave me alone, witch!" I cried, leaping away from her. In two bounds, I was on the other side of the clearing and up a tree. "I know what you've been doing and you won't get away with it!"

"Oh really?" cackled the witch. "I already did! I've got all your friends and I'm going to get you!"

She pulled out a potion from her robe and threw it at me. I dodged to one side, the potion narrowly missing my body.

I spun a silk thread and swung away through the trees. I couldn't risk the witch capturing me, but at least now I knew where she lived and the spiders had to be somewhere nearby. I was going to save my friends!

Day 23

I spent all day hiding from the witch. I'd found a little hollow in a tree barely big enough to squeeze all my legs into, but it gave me a good view over her hut so that I could keep track of where she was.

She didn't seem to have a clue where I was. I knew that she could smell me, but the boggy stench of the swamp seemed to hide my scent, so although she walked past my hiding place a couple of times, she didn't spot me lurking there.

At last, night fell and the witch retired to her hut. I waited until the lights went out before finally creeping out of my hiding hole.

My legs were stiff and cramped and I stretched them out one by one, trying to ignore the aches and pains shooting through them. However badly I felt, it was nothing compared to how the other spiders must be feeling, locked up waiting for a witch to harvest their eyes.

Where was she keeping them?

I edged towards the hut, making sure I kept to the shadows in case the witch was only pretending to be asleep. As I drew closer, I heard the sound of snores coming from inside. Either she was a really good actress or she was genuinely fast asleep.

First of all, I looked underneath her hut in case there was a basement she could conceal the spiders in.

Nothing.

I went behind her hut, thinking that the reason why she was trying to get me inside was to push me into a cage attached to the back.

Wrong again.

I paused for a moment, biting my lip as I wondered where the spiders could be.

"Hey! Stop squashing me!"

I jumped at the sound of the voice and as I did, I noticed that the ground where I'd been standing was covered in leaves, yet there wasn't a tree nearby. Brushing away a few of the leaves, I uncovered a metal bar.

I'd found them!

I started frantically digging away, uncovering the top of a cage filled with spiders.

"Zed? Are you in there?"

"Boris! Thank goodness. How did you find us?"

"A combination of luck and determination I guess," I shrugged. "That's not important anyway. What matters now is that I get you out of here. How does this cage open?"

"The witch has locked it," Zed told me. "She keeps the key inside her hut."

"The hut where she's fast asleep," I muttered grimly. "All right. I'm going to set you free. You guys wait here."

"Where else would we wait?" asked Zed, as I covered the cage back up, trying to make it look exactly the way it used to. If the witch knew that I'd discovered the spiders, she'd go mad. I didn't fancy fighting a witch on the rampage.

"I'll be back tomorrow, I promise," I whispered, as I wondered how on earth I was going to get the key away from the witch.

Day 24

Safely tucked away in my hiding spot, I waited for the witch to leave the hut the next morning. She wasn't a morning person and the sun was high in the sky before she emerged from her home.

"I'm going to find you today, Boris!" she called out, coming dangerously close to my tree, but she still didn't see me as she headed off into the swamp, looking up at the tree branches to try and find me. It didn't seem to occur to her that I was lying low this time – literally!

As she trotted off down a path deep into the swamp, I decided that now was as good a time as any to go to her hut. I didn't know how long she would be gone, but I knew that she wasn't inside right now and this might be my only chance at getting the key to the cage. She didn't seem to realize that I'd discovered the other spiders, so with any luck, the key would still be in her hut.

Pulling myself out of the tree, I crept across the swamp to her hut, trying to move as silently as possible. Going up the stairs, I pushed at the door to the hut, but it didn't budge.

Locked!

Well, I was a resourceful spider and a locked door wasn't going to stop me. I walked all round the hut and soon found what I was looking for.

An open window.

Spiders are very squishy and we can fit into tiny gaps if we want to. It was how I'd been able to squish myself into the tree trunk. The window might be small, but it was just big enough for me to be able to fit through.

I climbed up the wall and to the window. Taking a deep breath, I forced myself through the opening, one leg at a time. It was a tight fit, but at last I was through and standing inside the witch's home.

She wasn't exactly a tidy person, and I gingerly tiptoed through the hut, trying not to trip over the debris all over the floor. I plundered through drawers and looked inside cupboards, but I could have kicked myself when I saw the key hanging up on a hook by the door in plain sight. I should have known that the witch was too arrogant to think she'd need to hide it. It wouldn't occur to her that a spider might break in and rescue his friends.

I snatched it off the hook and went to open the door when I heard a sound that made me freeze. Footsteps!

There wasn't enough time for me to squeeze through the window before she came in, so with a mighty leap, I jumped up to the ceiling and clung to it with all my might.

The door opened and Louise walked in.

"Stupid spider," she muttered. "Like I needed his eyes anyway. I've got plenty of his friends locked up and once I've invaded the dungeon, he'll have to live with the fact that his family is gone and it's all his fault."

She left the door wide open as she walked over to a cupboard where she kept her potions, so I quietly let myself down and tiptoed down the stairs.

Rushing over to where the cage was buried, I uncovered it and fitted the key in the lock.

"Come on, everyone," I urged. "We don't have much time. As soon as the witch notices that the key's missing, she'll be after us, so we need to get going."

The spiders didn't need any encouragement to get out of the cage and they climbed out, happy to be free once more.

"My key!" the witch screeched, her voice echoing around the swamp.

"RUN!" I yelled, as she rushed out of the hut, potions in hand.

Spiders scattered in all directions as the witch threw splash potion after splash potion at us.

"Take that, you evil hag!" shouted Zed, throwing himself at her. He kicked her right in the chest, knocking her back into the hut, where she hit her head on the side of a table and fell to the floor, unconscious.

"Let's get out of here," I cried. "The witch knows where the dungeon is and she's told her friend. We have to warn the others before they attack."

The spiders all gathered together and set off out of the swamp, running as fast as our legs would carry us. The battle for freedom wasn't over yet.

Day 25

Do you know how fast a spider can run? It's very, very fast, especially when they know there's a witch coming up behind them, trying to destroy their entire colony.

When I'd left the dungeon, I hadn't known which way to go to look for Zed, so I'd wasted a lot of time wandering around, trying to find clues to where he'd gone. This time, I knew exactly where I was going and I was going to take the most direct route to get there.

We ran all morning and most of the afternoon before stopping for a quick break to get our breath back and have something to eat. Zed came to sit next to me.

"I'll never be able to repay you for rescuing me," he said. "Once the witch captured me and shoved me in with the other spiders, I thought that was it. I couldn't imagine anyone finding us down in that cage. When you found us, I couldn't believe how lucky we were. What made you decide to come looking for me? I didn't think anyone would miss me."

"Really?" I smirked. "What gave you that idea? Is it the fact that you've been giving newly spawned spiders stupid names and it's finally catching up with you?"

Zed blushed. "Look, about that. I'm sorry-"

I waved a leg to silence him. "Don't worry about that now. We've got bigger things to think about. Anyway, it's thanks to your tricks that I came to get you. I knew that a spider as naughty as you wouldn't just disappear like that. There had to be something else going on. So it's really thanks to you that we're going to be able to save the dungeon and all the spiders living there."

I pulled myself up.

"Speaking of which, we should hit the road again. I know we're all tired, but we've got to get back to the dungeon before the witch finds it. It's the only way we can save the spiders. Come on everyone. Let's go!"

In an instant, the spiders were all back on the road, running as fast as their legs would carry them, leaping off trees and using silk thread to swing from branches to get over obstacles. Nothing was going to get in our way.

Day 26

At last, we were standing in front of the entrance to the dungeon.

"It doesn't look like the witch is here yet," I observed. "Once we get inside, block the door up with cobwebs. It'll make it harder for the witch to break through."

"Got it," nodded a couple of spiders, starting to spin webs to barricade the door shut.

I led the way into the dungeon network and spotted a spider scurrying past.

"Hey! You! Go fetch Fang and the others and tell them to meet me in the conference room," I ordered. "We've got some important news for you all."

The spider hurried off to gather up the rest of the colony and soon they were all gathered in the largest room in the network, waiting to hear what I had to say.

"Listen up!" I called, as the spiders fell silent. "I've got some good news and some bad news. The good news is that I uncovered a plot by witches to capture all the spiders and harvest our eyes."

"Harvest our eyes?"

"No!"

"That's horrible!"

The room erupted into shouts and protests and I had to yell to be heard.

"I said it was good news!" I exclaimed. "I rescued all the spiders the witch had imprisoned."

"So what's the bad news?" called a spider from the back of the room.

"The witch knows where the dungeon is and she's on her way here now to capture us. We need to get the dungeon ready. If she thinks the spiders are going to be an easy victory, we're going to teach her a lesson she'll never forget!"

Day 27

Everywhere you looked, spiders were rushing around, setting up traps and building barriers to try and stop the witch when she attacked.

"How's it going, Gilbert?" I greeted, seeing him attaching a web across a corridor.

"Good, good," he nodded. "I don't think the witch will be expecting spider webs."

"Er…" I didn't have the heart to tell him that if you were going into a spider colony, the one thing you would definitely expect would be spider webs. He'd worked so hard on such an impressive web that I didn't want to destroy his morale.

"What are we going to do if the witch throws potions at us?" Gilbert asked.

"Duck out of the way, I guess. She's thrown a few splash potions at me and she hasn't managed to hit me once. She's a terrible shot!"

"That helps," laughed Gilbert.

"Hey, Boris. We've made some spider decoys. Want to come and have a look?" Fang called me over to where a group of spiders had spun webs in the shape of spiders.

"Those are amazing," I beamed. "There you go, Gilbert. That answers your question about splash potions. If we hide behind the decoys, any potion will explode harmlessly on the decoys so we can then rush the witch."

"She won't know what hit her!" cheered Gilbert. I hoped that he was right.

Day 28

I crouched behind a decoy spider, nervously watching the entrance to the dungeon. Our scouts had reported the witch coming this way and she wasn't alone. Hyacinth was with her.

"We can do this," I called to the other spiders. "Two witches aren't any scarier than one. It just gives us two targets to hit."

BANG! BANG! BANG!

I jumped at the sound of someone banging on the door. The web we'd put up to hold it in place was doing a good job, but it was only a matter of time before the witches broke through.

"Hold steady, everyone," I ordered. "You know the plan. Don't lose your nerve now."

BANG! BANG! CRASH!

The door flew open, revealing Louise.

"Come, my pretties. Let's not waste any time. Why don't you save us all a lot of trouble and surrender now? You know I'm just going to win the fight anyway."

She jumped down into the corridor, followed by Hyacinth. Pulling out a splash potion, she raised her hand, getting ready to throw it.

"Here, spidey, spidey, spidey." Louise called out to us, but nobody was foolish enough to leave their hiding place.

"All right. You want to do it the hard way. That's fine by me. It's more fun!" She turned to Hyacinth. "You go down that corridor and I'll go this way. If you see any spiders, you know what to do."

"Got it," nodded Hyacinth, trotting off in the direction Louise told her. I couldn't help but giggle when I heard her shriek when she walked into the web Gilbert had strung across the corridor.

"Get this stuff off me!" she spluttered. "It's all sticky!"

"Stop moaning!" Louise yelled back at her friend, but a moment later, it was her turn to scream when she fell through a floor trap and into a large ball of web, holding her in place.

"CHARGE!"

I gave the order to attack and spiders swarmed out of the walls, dropping down on the witches.

"Get off! Leave me alone!"

The two witches screamed and struggled to get their potions out, but the webs held them tightly in place and we were safely shielded by the decoy spiders as we kicked and hit the witches.

"Stop! Please stop! You're hurting me!" begged Louise.

"Why should we stop? You were going to steal our eyes," I pointed out. "You were going to destroy our entire colony. You don't deserve mercy. We should finish you right here and now so that you can't hurt any more spiders."

"Please don't!" pleaded Hyacinth. "This was all Louise's idea. I was just trying to help a friend. I didn't know what she was planning, honest I didn't!"

"Enough," said Fang, as the spiders began to attack again. "We're spiders. We're better than this. I think the witches have learned their lesson. We're not going to sink to their level."

I just managed to restrain myself from hitting the witches one more time, but it was tempting. Very, very tempting.

"All right," I said. "We'll let the two of you go, but it's on two conditions."

"Anything! Anything!"

"First of all, you promise never to use any spider parts in your potions."

"No spider parts?" gasped Louise. "But they're essential to so many potions!"

"I don't care. You find an alternative or you just don't make those potions. Either way, you're never going to hurt a spider again just to cast your spells."

"All right," said Louise grumpily. "I promise."

"Me too," echoed Hyacinth. "What's your other condition?"

"That you leave this place and never come back," I ordered. "You swear that you will never tell anyone else the location of our home and you will also warn everyone what will happen if they come into a spider lair."

"What will happen?" asked Louise.

"RAAR!" I roared in her face. Louise paled and her and Hyacinth turned and fled.

"Good riddance!" I called after them, as all the spiders cheered. We were safe at last.

Day 29

Fang and I were relaxing in the lounge area. "Yesterday was a good day, wasn't it?" Fang asked. "I had a lot of fun fighting off the witches. I'm glad things are quiet again now though. That was a little too much excitement for me!"

"I've been thinking about that," I replied. "I don't think we can really trust the witches to keep their word. I don't think we should stay here anymore. I've heard that there are other dungeons out there. I think we should go and find somewhere else to live so if Louise and Hyacinth ever do come back, they'll find an empty colony. I've been chatting to some of the other spiders and they all agree. We should leave."

"I hear what you're saying," Fang nodded, "and I can understand if the younger spiders want to leave with you, but I'm staying here. This is my home and it always will be. If the witches do come back, we've still got all the traps in place and I can fight them off. Think of me as your first line of defense if you like. With all the decoy spiders, Louise will never know that the rest of you have left."

"Are you sure? I'm really going to miss you."

"I'm sure," Fang told me. "And anyway, it's not as though you're never going to come and visit, is it?"

"Are you kidding? Try keeping me away!"

Day 30

I turned to look back at the entrance to the dungeon one last time.

"Don't be sad, Boris," Zed told me. "You've saved the spiders and now you're going to lead us to a new haven. I knew that I'd done the right thing when I gave you that name."

"Speaking of which, why *did* you call me Boris?" I asked. "I followed you to the swamp to ask you and didn't get the chance, thanks to all the excitement with the witches."

"Really? You saved me because I gave you a silly name?" Zed laughed. "Wow. My idea worked even better than I thought!"

"What idea?" Gilbert came over to join us.

"It's simple," Zed explained. "I give spiders silly names to help give them the strength to overcome any challenge. If you can deal with spiders making fun of your name, you can cope with just about anything and you've just proven me right."

"Yeah, well, all the courage in the world wasn't going to make me put up with what you lumbered me with," sniffed Gilbert.

"What was your name?" I asked. "Please tell me. I promise I won't laugh and I won't tell anyone."

Gilbert thought for a moment before shrugging. "All right," he said. "I'll tell you. Zed called me Patty. My name was Patty O'Furniture"

"Patty O'Furniture?" I couldn't help myself. I burst out laughing.

"Don't be mean," chided Zed. "That was a perfectly decent name. It's a name with Irish roots. It means powerful, strong, and durable. I knew that he'd grow into it."

"I prefer Gilbert," muttered Gilbert.

"You're right," I agreed. "Gilbert is a much better name for you. And I'm sorry for laughing. I don't blame you for changing your name after Zed played such a cruel trick on you. And I promise I will never tell another soul what Zed called you."

As we carried on through the forest, looking for a new dungeon to live in, I thought about how funny life could be sometimes. Zed and Gilbert had been mean to me and now we were the best of friends. Together, we were going to build a brand new spider colony where spiders could live in peace and safety.

46541093R00046

Made in the USA
Middletown, DE
02 August 2017